Dragging Anchor

Dragging Anchor

Keri Marinda Smith

Hanging Loose Press
Brooklyn, New York

Published by Hanging Loose Press, 231 Wyckoff Street, Brooklyn, New York
11217-2208. All rights reserved. No part of this book may be reproduced without
the publisher's written permission, except for brief quotations in reviews.

www.hangingloosepress.com

Printed in the United States of America
10 9 8 7 6 5 4 3 2 1

Hanging Loose Press thanks the Literature Program of the New York State Council
on the Arts for a grant in support of the publication of this book.

Some of these poems have appeared in the *Inquisitive Eater* and on Discipline Press,
as well as in *Hanging Loose* magazine. A special thanks to Donna Brook and Thomas
Moody for their help editing my work, and for everyone at Hanging Loose Press
for their support.—KMS

Cover art: *Absinthe Drinker* by Jayne Holsinger, gouache on paper, 11" x 7.5." From
the collection of Jane Augustine.

Cover design: Marie Carter

ISBN 978-1-934909-55-3

Library of Congress cataloging-in-publication data available on request.

Table of Contents

For Gainesville

Dragging Anchor

When a sailboat drags anchor you wake up in your berth you wake up with the wood around you but you know something isn't right you're still in your berth but it's like when you sleep with someone for many nights and when they turn you turn with them and when they breathe you breathe with them when they get up in the night you feel that they're missing and you know something isn't right

so you wake up in your berth and you feel the wood around you and the smell of canvas which isn't just salt air or age or sunlight it's sails that carry those things but also time

you know the smell it's the smell that all your father's sweaters had and all the beach towels laid out for you in the summer it's the smell of years on the boat but also something else

you're in your berth and there's the wood and the canvas but also the sense of time passing, too quickly, maybe you see the stars moving too but mostly you just feel it, so you get up and leave everyone else asleep you go outside and even in the middle of the summer there will always be that first chill of you alone, above deck, with the rest of the world sleeping and you see that the bow has turned around the wrong way starboard so you pull up the chain and it's so easy, so light in your hands, and you pull it in and feel the boat really pull with the current now, it could just float so easily out to sea but you look forward and set the anchor the other way left to the channel and wait for the anchor to catch and it does—the boat makes a small tug and you're awake and everyone is still sleeping so why not slip

into the water with the chain, hold onto it and let your body also float along with the current, held against the steady weight of the anchor and see all the little creatures around you light up like magic, your mom taught you the word, *phosphorescence*

your first moment that you can remember that was completely yours and years later your mother is remarried and you aren't in a ship but in a small house on another river and you want to go into the town to buy pickles so you ask your mom if you can drive and you're driving and you ask about the journals, the years you all spent sailing, and why her voice isn't there and why you can't read them, and it's not the first time you asked and she says

I burned them

it terrifies you and you're afraid to ask and you think about nights you spent awake at night alone, other nights where you're sure someone should have been awake and who knows

what really happened

but your mother is remarried and you like him so you all have dinner together in that little house on the river and at night you go to bed and you hear the wind howl and it's a sound you almost remember and early in the morning she calls your name and you answer, that's a sound
familiar like the wind, pushing against wood, against canvas, pushing the body of a boat out to sea

the wind on the river is different, fierce and Northern and it carries with it the smells of evergreen trees and the mating calls of Loons, their red eyes glowing on the river which you can see from your small window in the house, so like a ship

and you wake up in the middle of the night to its sounds and walk downstairs and the rest of the house is sleeping and still and you know that it's impossible for a whole house to drag anchor

Fourteen

It's hard to explain from pictures
but honey I used to be bad

sneaking out of the house barefoot
using the roof

any way to keep a door from opening
the kind of bad that was

out all night in the humidity
hanging out with the ocean and

whoever was around
which is to say

not bad at all just lonely
then when I figured out

I didn't have to be
well then

I didn't have to sneak around
all the doors opened on their own

Looking

Even at sixteen I was looking
for someone tall enough, who would see me and want me,
want their fingers inside me, would see me arrive
in the marina, in the stable, in the dust in the roadside, leaning against a truck,
any place I went to, while I was looking for something to do,
and they would put down their oysters or their paper plates or the fried fish
or champagne or cheap beer
and put their hands on mine because I was better than
an afternoon wasted alone
fishing or staring off into space or trying to get the horses back into their pens
and even at sixteen I was better than a swim in a lake.

And when I left them in the early morning
or late chilly evening in Florida or Georgia or South Carolina
where it does get chilly in the evenings I was still looking
and when I left them I left the taste on their lips, fingers or thighs,
the taste of someone better than them.

Ocala

Out in the country. The real country. The middle of Florida, in the Ocala National Forest, where the only restaurant is a Kangaroo gas station. I could stay barefoot for a whole week and no one would notice. Humidity like a blanket. White sand and forest and Coca-Cola lakes. The guy that owned the ranch was a horse thief. He sold people horses and then took them back in the middle of the night and then painted them different colors. They would come back to the ranch and he would say oh no, you're mistaken. I think he was one of my dad's only friends, and we kept our horses there. I spent weekends at the ranch for a few years. I was twelve, then thirteen. We would ride our horses all day under the giant oak trees and through blonde fields and sometimes across lakes, and come out dripping and relieved from the summer heat. Horse dust in my mouth. The smell of horses in everything. Even now if I smell horses, driving through the country with the windows down I have this homesick feeling for them. Then I was just a kid, I thought it was normal and granted that I would spend my days and nights outside forever. When my dad would go to sleep I would walk around the little ranch. The black lake looked blacker, and even I knew better than to swim in it at night. Horses aren't afraid of snakes, they have a natural immunity. That's true. But they are afraid of hogs and pigs. Avoiding the lake, I would walk (barefoot) up the sandy road to the pasture and stay still, wait for the horses to come to me. We smelled each other. When I walked back to the little cabin I would hear them, very quietly though, walking along the pasture, following me. That was our friendship. Recognition and presence. I would go back and sit on the porch and listen to all the bugs. A whole world of creatures making one noise in the night. In the morning we would go ride out again, my dad usually leading the way trying to find some trail he made up in his head. In the afternoons it might rain and I would walk to where the horses were just to see the steam coming up off them, to put my head against their necks and rub their wet hair, both of us probably thinking: I am here.

I Was a Teenage Horse Girl

the afternoon starts with Taco Bell
from the Kangaroo gas station
down the street
it's connected
the dirt road three miles
then the two lane county road
I only see one truck
and no one else
except Debra behind the counter
this is probably a Sunday

on the way back I walk along the bridge
over deep Coca-Cola river water
by the Blackwater Inn
where we might eat tomorrow
the only place with cheeseburgers
in about thirty miles
the rest is just
forest and spiders and horse trails

where are you
why am I wandering alone
in this place
this sad excuse for a ranch

I'll read by the lake
until the sun dips a little
then take Penny out riding
under oak trees
when the sky looks like her hair
we will head back together and after
she'll watch me swim in the green pool
surrounded by frogs and
other summer creatures

We Of That Time

Austin and I got tattooed when we were eighteen because we were worried that if I moved out of our little beach town we'd never see each other again never see each other walking down the beach after being up all night after telling our parents we were at each other's houses which always worked just to sneak into a punk show and then kill a few hours in an all night diner and then watch the sun rise up on the Atlantic after years of hanging out on my roof talking about all the bands we'd start one day and years of terrible awkwardness and first times with drugs and we didn't want to forget so we got a little outline of Florida on the backs of our legs with two words *remember when* and I graduated and I don't exaggerate when I say I never went back not even to spend the night with my mom who eventually left that little beach town too and then in a few years Austin followed me to Orlando and we got a house together in a boring part of town and started a punk band and it took us up and down the East Coast where we met people from all of the world who had never even heard of our little beach town and we drove up and down so many highways and the songs we wrote together connected us to all these people and we played festivals and small college towns and Austin fell in love and settled down in Gainesville so after college I followed him up there too and we worked in restaurants and lived under the beautiful oak trees that town is known for and rode our bikes around and started having a different time that would be punctuated by heartbreak because that's just what comes with those times but we had each other and hardwood floors and cheap rent and a green backyard and Austin didn't want to forget so he got the words from a Neruda poem across his chest *nosotros los de entonces* and we started different bands that played shows together and we put out a 7" EP with three songs from his band and three songs from mine and I would walk down the street to his house and drink wine all night and we would think about how far away we were from where we started and might be someday soon so that now while he's still playing music in that quiet town that can be so loud I can ride the train to the beach in far Brooklyn and read Neruda and think of us together then

In the Panhandle

The frozen crab legs
and artichoke dip
and french fries.

Endless Chardonnay
on the porch at dusk
and a cigar

and my stepmom sneaking off
to call her daughter,
who she never speaks about.

The pool, unused and warm,
the sound of frogs calling out around the yard
and the ocean, a few blocks away, also making its call.

In the morning the drive to the liquor store
for more wine and my dad listening
to baseball scores on the radio.

Nothing to talk about
except for the weather
and what we might want for dinner.

Last Swim

My mom moved away from Melbourne,
but I remember our last swim there
from the last time I visited. In late August,
with the windows down in the car
driving south on A1A, only I don't know
the name of the state park where we went
into the water, only the surprise I felt
seeing my mom in so little clothing,
and so sexual! So beautiful still in her 60's,
and not a bad surprise, just a quiet adjustment,
what animals must feel in the dark
when they think they're alone and instead discover
another body sleeping quietly near.

This Was When

I came up to Gainesville
before I lived there
when Leanne had that insane bird
that would fly out of the house and attack whoever walked by
this was when we went to the party at Ax Manor
when everyone was listening to Judas Priest
and I punched out all the ceiling tiles in the kitchen
this was when everyone knew all the words
to every song

this was when we all lived on the same block
four houses connected by a yard
when we built fires in late September
and did acid in the afternoons while we drank
cheap white wine
before we all started
to secretly really like Fleetwood Mac
this was when we spent all our free hours together
when we weren't washing dishes
when we were just playing music
when we were still writing the words
to every song

This Was Also When

I stayed up all night doing ecstasy for the first time and I loved it I remember listening to the Ramones on my small speakers alone in my room and feeling like my body was making the music like my body was actually producing the music and also writing the words whenever they were written but also now as they were being sung I was also writing them at the same time and I walked out of my house and the moon was up over oak trees and the light drifted down through the Spanish moss like bright and shining pollen and I saw my best friend stumbling home from the bar and he heard the words too and we saw each other and it was understood then how we would write the rest of the moment he started walking faster and I started walking faster and we ran into each other on the street at maybe one o'clock in the morning and we started making out to Needles and Pins and we pulled away laughing because we'd never kissed each other much less had a moment like that together and we kept laughing and whatever could have happened passed because I grabbed his hand and told him about the drugs and we walked back to the block where everyone lived and when I got there I tapped on another friend's window very quietly and he let me in and I lay down in his bed and he held me and talked me down and I told him how much I loved everyone but especially our friends and above all the Ramones

Southbound

I can't tell you how many times I've driven up and down 95,
or stopped at South of the Border, one time I even slept there.
Really, slept on the roof while the giant sombrero's neon light
shined down on me like an old blues song.

Highways are the best way to see the country. To feel its changes.
To emerge suddenly in a quiet, empty summer night
listening to Neil Young on the radio and feel completely
alone. The Gun Club have good songs for driving too. Inexplicable,
how I know the words to songs about driving around LA at night,
when I've never been. Yet there will always be people writing
haunted, lonely songs about driving and traveling and cement and even dirt roads
because people will always be driving, as long as there are cars,
and after that someone will make up some song about feeling lonely on a horse
again, when it comes to that,
if there are still horses,
and god, I really hope so.

Voodoo

We were huffing glue
from giant industrial cans
poured into shopping bags.
It dripped down between the floorboards
in the kitchen that still
had the spice smells of meals
cooked long ago,
when other people lived here.

I used to lie in bed here,
the mornings full of grey light that leaked
in between the crown of oak trees
that circled the house.

Now we stay up late
just to the sit on the porch
and watch the sparks
fly up from the fire
that will burn everything,
even the bottles,
even the spiders
that made their homes above you
and under the house
where a boy once took me, down in the dust
which he said was full of animal bones
the people that lived here practiced voodoo
I don't know why but I believed him at the time and
maybe they still do.

Practiced when voices carry out
into the night when the screen door stays open
or when the sound that's trapped in the brittle glass
of tube amplifiers that break in the cold, in the garage

then the house will once again
be filled up with our song.

Lost Jewelry

Long copper earrings high summer lost somewhere in Texas hotel room cold watching ex-boyfriend with his new lover asleep next to my cheap interstate bed. Delicate silver given from mother lent to a friend for a dance I went alone to. Turquoise I bought for myself and delicate vertebrae attached hung down between my breasts made me feel like a grown up it fell down the drain in the tub of my first apartment. One diamond from the ring my dad gave my mom on a sailboat in the middle of the Pacific Ocean. She managed to get it safely around the world and I got it worthless in no time. Black leather choker that always looked good with my blonde hair but I gave it to a friend with better cheekbones and a fiercer outlook on the world. Set of bangles collected at strip-mall stores around my tiny wrists. Broken hood ornaments of expensive cars collected in a basement and presented to me in soft rabbit fur they show up in pictures. Here's me in San Francisco and again in New York. How could I have lost that many bracelets in one year? Left on bright balconies and in shared apartments. A trail for me to follow.

Jet Set

She wears jewelry as second skin
tiny brittle bones and silver rings.
She puts her eyes on every night
and sleeps through the mornings.
She goes out to the desert and takes pictures
surrounded by a dusky expanse of nothing
has easy quotes about eternity,
rides horses down the dunes.
She has a loft and a spotted dog,
and poses in front of the mirror,
long and slender and balanced.
She's never worked a day in her life
and she's looking for a ticket out of here
to go somewhere warm when it's cold
and vice versa, black shawl in the airport.
She's thinking about Morocco. She's pale
and has the whole world at easy disposal,
it fits around her waist like everything else.

I Want to Give Up All My Enemies

even if it's just a message sent in the early hours
of Christmas morning as a way of saying I remember
we were close once around this time and even
if it's something trivial sent
on the occasion of a death even
the smallest gesture will be remembered
years from now why bother holding onto the slight
perceived or intended or deep heartbreak
a careless drifting apart
two people who found less and less to say
until the space manifested into something sour
something dark passed back and forth
a turned shoulder or a shut door
the weight of a non-invitation
but if we could begin to reverse this
to send out some kind of signal
some kind of pheromone of I'm sorry
here in this space
let me buy you a drink
forward you this message
or begin at some point to say

Be That As It May

I still believe her because
you didn't

did you when I said it?
I told you

you said well maybe
and possibly and

hopefully but
probably

now I say
be that as it may

I will choose to believe her
when she tells me.

A Love Song

I was wandering around the outskirts of your wedding
there were horses out in the field and I wanted them
to put their bristled noses in my hand
I was wearing this ridiculous pink dress and getting drunk
after the wedding you went off with your new wife
all the punks in town from Gainesville got beer
jumped the fence into the hotel pool
and I didn't have sex with my date but we still talk
I think a month later I moved to New York
I sent you poetry and you emailed me about your new daughter
we didn't talk I just sent you what I was working on
since you wrote me my letter of recommendation to get into grad school
since you'd written some of my favorite zines and essays
since I'd known you in high school but we had only met through your writing
and then later from bands you'd been in and shows we'd played together
I woke up about a year later but still in August
Ryan called to say you had killed yourself
I made the phone calls and sent out whatever words I could
another year later and I still like to read something you wrote called
a love song, anytime you can.

A Case for Not Doing Acid at the Beach

I'll already be experiencing
so many emotions
being home
handling all that sunlight
preparing to burn
but there are those spots
on my shoulders I need to get checked
I will have convinced myself they're cancer
before noon and I don't want to think about that
in the sun and Kirk will start thinking of LA
because Miami reminds him of home
except here he fits in so well
and I stand out
white on white sand
and he'll want to buy a ticket back there
or we'll stay forever
get a job bartending on the beach
shaking daiquiris for retired ladies all afternoon
I'll steal a car
end up in Publix
licking the floors out of gratitude.

Two Old Dogs

How did my dad become so square?
He put himself through Dartmouth, not rich,
an inevitable cowboy.
Races boats through college,
quit being a Federal prosecutor in Baltimore
to become a communist and sailed around the world
with my mom. Had me in South Africa hanging out
with apartheid protestors, bought a case of champagne for everyone
in the hospital when I was born.
He was always the one making jokes in bars,
making friends with strangers.
Years later he moved to the Panhandle, married his secretary
and now he sits on his porch, drinks two bottles of cheap Chardonnay
each day, gives away wishes on baseball games.
His dog has health care bills more expensive than mine,
and his cigars cost more than my shoes. I don't know what he's looking at
every night with he stares out across the lake
in front of their house and honestly I can't remember
how old he is.

When did my daughter go so wild?
She used to sit so quietly in the truck
when we pulled horses, pulled all nighters, when we drove
across the country. She used to open my Heineken on the boat,
sing along to all our favorite country songs.
She used to look forward to antique malls, to hours with the CB radio,
to visiting me and spending the day at the beach.
She was always so excited to travel. She moved to New York City
where she's probably out on the streets at night talking to *strangers.*
Probably listens to National Proletariat Radio every day
in her dirty apartment instead of calling. And I see
she went to Mexico again, why not visit me instead?
Our kitchen's clean. We invited her to Thanksgiving

a few years ago. She never came.
She didn't even come to my dad's funeral. She doesn't care.
She sends me pictures and letters I don't understand.
And each year that goes by
I forget how old she is.

Modern Love

My friend asks me out dancing
I insist on vodka and then tequila
we don't go out dancing as much now

when we lived in a small college town
we'd go out all the time
a few nights a week

there wasn't a lot to do and no one
to look cool for
we'd dance all night and then go home alone

tonight it's Friday in New York
and I wish I had nicer shoes
and she's still in her wheelchair and I'm bored

but when David Bowie starts singing
"Modern Love" I lean down to take her hands
and we dance the way we used to

On Court Street

There is a deli selling all kinds of smoked fish,
sandwiches, pickles and little jarred eggs tart condiments
on rye bread, soda water and coffee and down the street
there's a bookstore worth going to.

Farther along Atlantic Avenue there's a park,
under Brooklyn Heights by the water
and all kinds of things growing between rocks
which is where he will join me.

On this afternoon I'll go looking
for a spot in the shade with the wind coming up
off the East River where I will wait
for the only thing missing.

In the West Village

That well dressed guy shoulder-checked you
and called you a cunt right to your face.

You turned around, broad daylight
and said *excuse you* and damn if he didn't just hit you

so hard right across the face that you almost fell
into the basement of the flower shop, and the traffic cop

watched you get up and hit him back and said
lady you can't do that here like somehow

the man in the suit still yelling at all five feet of you
wasn't even there. I pulled you up and over to

the pizza place where our phones died
so we went to charge them at a bar so we could text our boyfriends.

Waiting there, we talked about men and women and at five o'clock
you got on the train and I walked out onto 6th Ave alone.

The Slaughtered Lamb

We meet up in a bar off West 4th St
and I realize
after the second beer
that it's the first time we've all been together
since Travis killed himself.

We talk about art, partners, plans for moving
or staying, and upcoming birthdays.

We are all further past 30 than we expected.

Everyone takes turns buying a round,
and the lights in the bar surround us
not like a crown, not like a halo.

I hug Ryan fiercely, he's on his way
to see his new girlfriend, the one he's visiting
who is his own age, a comic artist, promising.

Mike says he just wants one more beer
so that the bike ride over the bridge
goes by faster. I laugh

the whole way to my art show
where I don't know anyone.

June

Getting out of bed feels pointless,
untethered, out of context
like the wind hitting the building
like it might topple something around us.
Imagine what could collapse in the night.
I have dreams so vivid about a cat I used to own
I wake up with allergies.
I buy new blankets, drink different tea,
but each night it's the same and it's not really sleep.

After a week I decide to leave the house
by picking out a book to give to the barista
down the street who always remembers my name.
I get out of bed and carry the book for him
as precious as a ripe yellow tomato
handed over freely in wartime.

Left

what is left after $45 lipstick
trips to Paris in retirement
folded fur in the closet
and funerals

the books on the shelf
and my ability to understand them
familiar words comfort
in the end

after Kirk and clean laundry
long swims in bath water ocean
all you can eat crab legs
even the claws

Talking about the Weather

Remember feeling lonely
alone but in a good way like a self-contained body in the world
in the sunshine and wearing it the weather like a cape trailing behind
then really finding out what being alone was like, like fog in the bay
rolling in, cutting me off from the world and with only the echo of footsteps
in the streets for company. Then in the summer falling in love and maybe
finding new weather sticky like sugar like a lover like never being alone
not even at home especially not in the kitchen where the lover haunts
like dawn, always there and happiness but never alone.
Even the summer ends and it's the weather.
coming up off the ground, that promising chill of fall
and today the weather is like that, really the weather of being perfectly alone
but perfectly on the edge of it, not really alone but love is farther out off the coast
like other weather, a different feeling for me, alone.

Give Up for Spring

Hang up your used clothes
ignore getting them dry-cleaned
throw away boxes of photographs
maybe you'll see those people again
this summer and who cares about
all the stacks of paper who cares
about a final draft they're done
throw them out or send them off
they have to be done
give up for spring any chores you don't feel
like doing just get rid of as much as you can
leave one perfect coat
for yourself to take outside
and go watch the dogs in the park

In a Few Days an Inferno

the sun came out and it seemed that winter was over
then Cody got bone cancer and I went to visit him
took the bus from Chinatown to Philly and ate cheap dumplings alone

then Will died from drinking and pills intentional or who knows
and I talked to friends from all over the world and we agreed
that we were homesick and there was no remedy

the sun was still out and I went for a very long bike ride
around south Brooklyn and then took the ferry up to Greenpoint
and finished reading three books of poetry and a new Colombian novel

which I enjoyed but the way the author wrote about fear as a ubiquitous thing
seemed too real to me after being trapped in a retail store on 34th Street
where reports of a false shooting sent two hundred people running past me

I took dozens of pictures of the new flowers that were out in Park Slope
and wandered in and out of private gardens and made small donations
and graciously accepted a free dinner of bread and cheese from old friends

my stepdad had a stroke and after talking to my mom
and working nine hours in the bar I ate a cupcake that my friend brought me
and my boyfriend brought me home a very good bottle of Barbera

then the landlord told us they wanted to hike the month to month up
by almost a thousand dollars so we went out for more wine
and spent money on oysters that we can't afford but felt like we'd earned

Dan

You couldn't have known
when we first met that night drinking
cheap beer all night in Orlando
that seven years later
you'd take on the lease of my apartment
with the wraparound deck
under the chestnut trees in Gainesville
and that you
my most solitary friend
who reads all the Russian classics
would fall madly in love
with my cat
named Puppy
so that now when I call you from Brooklyn
we talk about books for awhile but
eventually you'll break down
and tell me about all the funny things he does
rolling around in the sunshine down there

In the Hospital

My stepdad had to relearn to swallow
the stroke broke up cells they either swelled
or emptied everything out of his brain
the blood either pouring in too fast
or not at all
it sounded like a lack
of oxygen and now he can talk
partially
but needs to be taught again
how to get out of bed
move his long legs around
swallow along
with the physical therapist
and my mom tells it all to me
in shaky breathless sentences
that string along and along
and while on the phone I think
tomorrow I'll bike down
to see the cherry blossoms

66 Degrees Today

I opened all the windows from the couch
collected bags of ice around my knee

imagined the roses opening up
in front of the houses along my street

corners I won't be seeing
green spaces where pockets of cool air

are gathering. Where
I won't be passing through

on my way to get coffee or walking
aimlessly because my old injury is back

again, so I've set myself up
toward the window imagining

what the day is like out there
where I can feel it coming in though

I cannot be outside enjoying
this brief moment of peace in July.

Wyckoff Street

I don't know what it's like
to be married.
Let alone live
with someone for that many years
but I like the feeling of the kitchen,
a whole complete place
a world for two, and three when I'm there.
The door opening for me,
coffee and I know where the milk is.

I see Donna fuss
about errands and doctor's appointments
and we all fuss about politics, left and further left,
changing places like dancers taking their turn...

I just want that look of anticipation,
when she's not paying attention
to me but staring out past the window

waiting for Bob to come home
when she interrupts us to shout
there is he, that's him, walking up now!

This Bus Has Been Checked for Sleeping Children

I imagine him
walking down the aisle between brown polyester seats
having his own daydreams
while the bus idles under diesel scented
chestnut trees, their leaves glowing
in this Boerum Hill afternoon,
his own early winter fantasy
as distant
as the damp bodies in the far back
limp and snotty, already sick
already planning on stolen hours
if they could sleep
when instead he lifts them up
by their shoulders
interrupted, now safe
and awake in the clear world.

The Kind of Person Who

Walking around with the sun out finally
I feel like the kind of person who
knows what kind of bagel to order
always the same request something
snazzy like toasted pumpernickel
instead of my panic and hesitation
between plain and everything
I feel like only ordering
a mezcal on the rocks at every bar
for the rest of my life! I will only own
three worn tee shirts and a perfect pair
of black jeans, $700 boots
I will go get my nails done, I will be the kind of person
who always looks ready to go out, at 9am or 11pm
I will be wearing earrings.
Oh my god, I could paint my room sky blue!

Thinking While You're at Work

I'll start wearing shirts with sailboats on them
maybe even grow my hair long,
relocate to the Keys
and spend my winters writing trashy novels
about all the lovers who weren't you. Or
I could dress myself in black, textures
and layers of the same cloth
which will remind you
of your dark nights spent
undercover in bars as someone
that belonged there
with someone else. In my mind there's
a magazine filled with all the women
I could be except this one,
me. Thankfully you
just love me simply
naked in your bed,
awake in the early morning
waiting for you to come home.

Smoked Meat

"It could be worse. It could be life without mortadella sandwiches."

Philip Levine let me tell you,
Montreal has the best sandwiches in North America.
I'm sure you've been, since you seem like the kind of guy
who would take the Amtrak a few hours to eat lunch,
and walk around some chilly city alone with a mustard stain
on your shirt. Just like us, like me and my friends coming down
off Mont Royale, when we decided we were just going to walk
down Saint Laurent and stop at every smoked meat restaurant
and deli counter until we hit the water, and we traded bites
back and forth while we walked, the saltiness and the dry bread
making us hungrier and hungrier, comparing those subtle flavors
of salt, vinegar and coriander, and then down at the water under
September sun we opened some very cold, very cheap beer
and I think you would have approved of the whole thing really.

At the Lake House

I think to myself
I could do this,
the short walk down
to the frozen water
to collect firewood,
to stand outside
with the trees and smoke.
In the evening there will be
a book, many glasses of wine,
some warm thing for dinner,
easy sleep in a cold bed.
But in a few days
I think I'd start remembering
bodega iced coffee, train lines
screeching at 2am,
and that cute bartender.
Cheap nachos, good drugs,
new shoes, used records,
art galleries, punk shows—

the woods and even
this house won't be enough for me.

Late Era Clash

While tattooing me Mike said
everyone's free to wage their arbitrary battles
while we talked about gentrification
he didn't mean the whole of Bushwick
or burning down condominiums
just that he wouldn't go to that new spot
on the corner
ever
I wanted a beer and went with my leg
all wrapped up and dripping it was August
and inside I saw all the white punks drinking
imported beer and I paid my tab went home
alone and kind of got what he meant

Ridgewood

But it's all here!
Look, the bike lane
but look, the whole neighborhood
of Ridgewood, I know in the '30s
was *for* Hitler, full of Germans
and fascists who would now be sad
would cry all night in their beers oh hell
let's imagine them crying even now
into every single street every intersection
all over Ridgewood even hopefully
into the hospitals where they are dying
and the cemeteries where they are already
dead. And that's how Ridgewood will be
and the people from Northern Mexico will be
hawking their drinks and their lunches
selling food and laughing and everyone
in the parks can be there
this summer.

Two and a Half Minutes to Midnight

My friends and I wait as long as possible to go to the dentist
it has to be under extreme duress before we ask around
about the cheap dental clinics, and thankfully I've been spared
I haven't been to the dentist in over ten years.
I have a weird rash on my feet, sometimes
I try looking it up on the internet, which makes me break out into hives.
If it wasn't for the nurses at Planned Parenthood I wouldn't have had access
to my birth control, blood tests, antibiotics (when needed) or peace of mind.
At least I'm not pregnant but the ocean floods the streets of Miami every day
at high tide and so my dreams of ever owning a house near the beach are futile and
I've been shitting blood for seven months now
but it makes more sense to buy antacids at Target before work
than to pay out of pocket to see a doctor, and which doctor?
Sometimes I don't know where to start. I bring home cheap beers
and read the paper, and in an interview Noam Chomsky says
it's two and a half minutes to midnight, referencing last century's doomsday clock
and I set my alarm for tomorrow and finish my beer and sleep easy
knowing that at least someone actually gets me.

Legs

The burgers are perfect in far Rockaway
and the water is usually just ok
I think we all go out for different reasons
my boyfriend likes the frozen drinks
and the little grasses on the dunes.
The sun is setting and people begin to pack up
I watch this girl on the beach with these long legs
like if you made a figure of a person using your hand
it would be all fingers
distracting me from my book which might be
contemporary Chinese poetry or Russian history
instead making me think of bicycles and horses
and the sometimes perfect machinery of our bodies
which is easy to think about in the summer when we aren't moving
and the sun becomes hidden under storms making their way in
making the afternoon suddenly cool when what made it all worth it—
an unobstructed view of the ocean.

Only Human

A guy passed me on the street but waited
until I had passed before he said hello
and I didn't respond, hurt he said
hey I'm a human
and yes, honey, you are
but you're going the wrong way
down Tompkins Avenue into the sunshine
under the green summer trees and it's 5 o'clock
on your day off probably and I'm human too
but heading to work where last week
one of my managers made me cry
for whatever misstep or miscalculation
and where for the next six to eight hours I'll think
about how my career hasn't started yet but if I'm lucky
I could work for a least forty more years at something
literally anything else but this thing that I'm on my way to do
so hello, keep going your own way into the afternoon
get an ice cream cone for me, sit in the shade somewhere
continue to be human, maybe take the train down to Coney Island
fall in love, brace yourself for the next few years or just July.

In The City

Today was a nice day for everyone, it seems
because everyone's around to get dinner tonight
two people that don't know each other but who will
get along over drinks, sitting outside. In a little bit
we'll all meet up because we're off work
today I took myself uptown and made it to 59th &
Lexington in 45 minutes, proud of that, time
for an iced coffee and made it to my appointment
for a free haircut, which turned out good, not too short
and then remembered exactly where the M train would be,
I knew it was there! Which took me to 14th where I got off
walked down past bars I used to hang out in during grad school
and hit the shade in Washington Square Park, after
another iced coffee I began to panic thinking
it's been ten years since I've been to the dentist
the constant nagging, thankfully distracted by my phone in my pocket
I beelined it for a friend's shop, said hello, arranged dinner
it's amazing what you get done, very cheaply, on a Wednesday.

Ordered Rest

I went to the ER late Saturday night they ordered rest
which means I won't have any money for rent next week
so for three days I have nothing to do but stare out the window
and think of reasons I could make up for mailing a check in late
It's New York so I think anything would probably work, like
I was arrested over the weekend, outstanding bench warrant
taken in until I could see the judge and pay for the old ticket, etc
it's a pretty familiar story. Except I'm white and could
probably afford bail, so I wouldn't sit in a cell for that long
not a few weeks or four months like some of the poor teenagers
at Rikers, twiddling their thumbs waiting for the judge, the court, somebody
to figure out what not having bail doesn't make them guilty
so anyway that excuse is out, but I still have three days
to sit on the couch and face the window, watch cars and young people
pass up and down my street, enjoying July, enjoying their week
and maybe they're worried about paying rent too
but have learned the kind of easy care that comes from knowing
somebody else, somewhere can figure it out but who could I count on?
No one I know has any money, we all work on our feet
but at least when I told my friends about my accident they came over
brought me a cane, cheap vodka, generic aspirin and some very good books.

For You, a Map

I like it when
you put both your belts around me.

Can't we just sit in the kitchen
and enjoy this apple, this sunshine?

Can't we just
sit down in the shower for a little while?

I don't know if I could possibly survive
another weekend with you.

Where will we go
when we are done being here together?

At some point I will have to go home again.
But at which point on the map, and whose map?

At some point I will make a map,
and you're on it as a destination.

Myself as Object

Let words go
let the form unfold
it's possible to give up
control

over yourself and the situation
let the shirt come off
the hands pulling the underwire of my bra
up over my head

and with the situation now happening
words won't be necessary after *yes*.

Is this an abstraction?
Let's insert some meaning.

I like the attention,
and you like to watch.

Find the form again,
I'm still in control of
this situation

give me the rope,
this is how I harness the structure
or whoever is in my mouth
and under me

we are not just objects
but beings with meaning
and can be both things
or more than two things
at the same time.

Message

I trick you into coming
to the show tonight by telling you
that I had a dream about you
it was the end of the world
but we were surviving
you agree to come
what I don't tell you is that
in the dream you put your tongue down my throat
and your tongue unfolded into me
it was miles long
and filled up my whole throat
my whole body
until I woke up
and I responded

There's Many Places

in New York to feel alone,
I think the bike rides through Bed-Stuy
and Crown Heights make you feel
isolated because down there
everyone is pretty busy, and won't look
twice at you even when you're on a bike
in the sunshine on your way to the Green-Wood Cemetery
with its cathedral trees and old stray cat smells
(it's the grass) and it's not that everyone's dead
it's just that there's only one way out of that place
and it's a long way back. If you take the ferry
over to the city you can pretend to window shop
through either Village but keep going
south of Houston and down Forsyth
into Chinatown at night, on a Sunday,
and see two groups of women
twenty or so in each, dancing to slow music
and in conformity, then you feel it well up before
leaking around you like the orange lights of the park.

Cortisone Reaction

I have a hard time
with protesting and voting and meetings
because I think I know at this point
in my life that the only thing that will change anything
is blowing up a federal office, and robbing banks
to pay for guns and for safe houses. And they did that
already, all over the world in the '60s and '70s and
what did we get instead? Neo-liberalism. The FTAA.
I painted a banner. I wanted to hang it from a bridge.
I think someone did eventually, and someone will
do everything eventually. But I just stay home lately
and pick all my scabs at once, and watch
the blood run down my legs in different directions.

Places That Scare Me

The dark eyes of my friend's babies
perfect and shining almonds
unblinking like they know me
recognizing my shape as someone safe
but I can't imagine belonging to anything
like that, being a part of something
so completely, it actually grosses me out
the thought of my cervix dilating
the umbilical cord pulling, the placenta
sliding out of me after, I see it all
in their non-eyelashes, in their symmetrical heads
but even I can admit they have an otherworldly smell
that makes me think of the empty husk
of the blue whale's heart on display
in that museum, pale and delicate
but it could withstand the pressure
of the deep and lightless ocean.

How at night when I'm alone I remember
footsteps up and down staircases
in houses I'll never visit again
places I cannot go to and things
I don't want to spend time with because
they'll make me want to live inside them forever.

So You Wanted

to see the pollen drifting down
covering wood floors
porches
bicycles
even
the surface
of the rivers
through the most central of the state

a yellow film

that clings to the skin
when surfacing
along the little hairs
over the small of your back
and arms blonde
into neon
what you don't see

on a Saturday night now

crying on the subway
big sobs
deluge of homesickness
4am gotta get home
any way
you can

How I Got Here

growing up I was alone on the ocean
with myself up at night on autopilot
cruising south off the Atlantic coast
I knew something was out there

later I remember the feeling
uncontrollable like the tide toward the moon
and I began to write the words down
and my mom's voice asking me to read them out loud
and then again

on Grandfather Mountain up in the foggy air
that same sharp feeling like being out
on the ocean that same pull
I had to write it down and write it down again

in high school with books and records
lying face down against the carpet
with the open window
and the humid southern air coming in
turning cool I didn't know how good I had it
all that time with nothing to do but read
and feel sorry for myself

sleeping with Lorca in college
the book always in my bed or in my backpack
and going to Spain to write long poems
about churches and dusky-eyed women
who fell in love with men on horses and
I drank whiskey and rode motorcycles
for the first time and began to find
my own voice

years of writing music for other people
and writing for myself privately
long nights on the road in vans traveling
the country and long stretches of time when
I didn't write anything just celebrated
being alive and aimless in the world
with my wild tribe of friends and lovers
to keep company and the occasional
night to write about

reading Paz in Mexico hitchhiking
and writing about clear water about
green mountains about the calls of
foreign animals and little towns
not knowing the language but learning
the gestures and how to sit with coffee
still on the busy mornings of others

finding the same labyrinth in Argentina
the same cobbled streets and shops of leather
like the old libraries I knew from Borges
and I drank wine solo and called my mom
from a payphone and she said
describe it for me again

years when I became obsessed
with orange street lights and humidity
I cared less about heartache or even myself
just oak trees and the smells of horses
coming across the lakes and I thought
it was finally where I belonged

I couldn't write when I was in love
because I was bored and then I couldn't
write when I was heartbroken because
I was drunk for six months

so I started looking for new experiences
and landscapes and scenes
that I could capture

waking up in the hotel in Oakland
covered in bruises happy strung out no
plans just a weekend well spent and
waiting to hear if the next year would be different
and I got the call to come to New York to grad school cried
in the airport and told my mom and she said
tell me again and again

writing all night at an open window and
not feeling lonely because just outside
are coffee shops and bars and bookstores
and all the places I've come to call home
and writing for myself and for others
in taxi cabs coming over the bridge
over the sparkling dirty river
after working all night and waking up
cold in a cheap apartment finally getting
to write for the first time
about snow